Whatever It Takes

A Young Mother's Quest to Survive Tragedy

By

Dayna Gfeller-Mackley

© 2003 by Dayna Gfeller-Mackley. All rights reserved.

No part of this book may be reproduced, stored in a retrieval system, or transmitted by any means, electronic, mechanical, photocopying, recording, or otherwise, without written permission from the author.

ISBN: 1-4107-1168-4 (e-book)
ISBN: 1-4107-1169-2 (Paperback)

This book is printed on acid free paper.

1stBooks - rev. 03/20/03

Dedication~

This book is dedicated in loving memory to my daughter Tasha, whose death opened up a part of me that had been hidden away for many years. Her death forced me to search for answers to questions that most people don't know exist. In this quest to find answers- I stumbled on to much more. I found myself.

Table of Contents

Dedication~ iii

Introduction~ vii

One~ Dreams or Reality? 1

Two~ The Early Years 4

Three~ Creating Our Life 11

Introduction~

This is a story about lessons I've learned throughout my life. I firmly believe that God creates each of us and sends us to this earth to learn things that can only be learned by living and experiencing the true happiness, as well as the devastating heartache that lifes' situations tend to bring about. Several things that life has taught me are very simple....*Live every day to it's fullest potential because tomorrow is promised to no one. *Live cautiously, but not too careful....if you live everyday being 'careful' - you miss too many things in life that could have brought even more happiness. *Don't, for one minute, think that you are in control of your life- God, and only God, is strong enough to be capable of that. *I've also learned that you should tell the people in your life that you love most, how you feel, every single day-never miss an opportunity to share love. *Never save *anything* for a special occassion- for every day that you are alive is special . *And probably one of the simplest mottos to live by is: *I know not what the future holds, but I know Who holds the future.*

One~ Dreams or Reality?

Two of my earliest childhood memories came to me in recurrent dreams. These dreams dictate the deaths of my grandfather and my great grandfather. I was 38 when I started having these recurrent dreams. After the same sequences were repeated over and over in my sleep, I questioned my grandmother and other family members about the incidents.

The first 'dream' was of the death of my dad's father- Grandpa Harold. In my dream I follow a little girl. She is at my great grandmother's house in Colorado [where I visited frequently growing up]. Breakfast was ready and the little girl was asked to go upstairs and wake Grandpa, who had apparently slept later than usual. In this dream I follow her, a very young girl [2-3 years of age], as she climbs a tall, steep, uncarpeted staircase with walls on both sides. At the top of the stairs she makes a turn to the left, entering the second door where the grandpa is asleep. The little girl playfully bounces upon her sleeping grandfather to wake him. He doesn't wake. He had died in his sleep.

The second memory, also a recurring dream, unfolds at about the same time, involving the same little girl. This time she is at Grandma Helen's house in Kansas [where I was raised]. In this dream, the frightened little girl is sitting at the top of the stairs, looking out the glass door which leads into the garage. It seems to be around late afternoon or early evening, or possibly, on an overcast day as it looks dreary through the glass window to the outside. The little girl waits patiently for her grandma to return. As the light blue car pulls into the shadow of the garage, the little girl is still sitting at the top of the stairs. She is afraid to move her eyes from the door to the bottom of the stairs opening into the basement. At the bottom of the stairs lay the motionless body of her great grandfather on the concrete floor. He had fallen down the stairs. The little girl was waiting for someone-anyone-so she wouldn't be afraid anymore. Great grandfather never woke from the deep coma and died six months later.

I have since learned that this little girl was me. I was around the age of three. I had a difficult time imagining why I would dig up these memories, and more important, where did they come from?

In the past few years of my life, many things have become much clearer to me. Memories that had been tucked away-deep inside me somewhere, have made their way to the surface. I am finding out, and beginning to believe, that our lives are broken into small fragments, much like a

Whatever It Takes

puzzle. Each piece being designed to fit into place at the precise moment to complete one complex image when our life on this earth is over. Only God is to know what the finished image is supposed to look like. Every day in our life lays one more piece of this master puzzle into place.

Dayna Gfeller-Mackley

Two~ The Early Years

This particular puzzle [my life] began in 1963. I was born early in the morning on April 30, to a young, outgoing, popular couple who had their whole future ahead of them. Dennis Gfeller and Diana Wagoner had grown up in separate communities in northwest Kansas only 23 miles apart. They played together as toddlers and young children. In May 1962 they married and created a family with two daughters, Dayna and Darla, born 19 months apart. I was the oldest of the two and neither of us would ever know how unique our lives were until many years later.

On July 31, 1965, the young couple died instantly in a fiery corvette crash just five miles from their home, orphaning me and my 8 month old sister. Neither of us remember this chapter of our lives as we were both so young. We were taken in to live with and be raised by dad's parents- Grandpa Harold and Grandma Helen. Mother's parents-Grandpa George and Grandma Toni also had a hand in raising their only grandchildren of their only daughter. Looking back, both sets of grandparents as well as other extended family members made my sister and I feel so loved and wanted that we never really missed our biological parents or felt that our lives were, in any way, different from any of the other children that we were exposed to growing up.

For myself, it wouldn't be until some 35 years later, when a devastating accident would make it more than clear to me, exactly what was taken from me that early morning in 1965. Also, making me aware of just how unique and abnormal my life really is.

The death of my parents at such a young age created a different life for everyone in the family. Grandparents had to once again become "parents" for Darla and I. Our primary caregivers became Grandpa Harold and Grandma Helen. Their daughter (Dad's sister) Debbie was 8 years old-six years older than myself-so we had an older, sister-like companion in her. My dad's younger brother, David, was married. He and his wife Judy had began their family with Kent, their first son, who was born in February before my parent's accident.

Shortly there-after is where my first memory [dream] was created. Grandpa Harold suffered a fatal massive heart attack on October 4, 1966 while we were visiting Grandma Helen's parents in Colorado. Again, I was too young to recall any of the events that followed his death. I assume we were probably protected from enduring the pain and loss of the situation. However, I am quite sure, now, that we had to have sensed a major difference in our lives at this time, much as we probably had to have experienced at the time our parents abruptly disappeared from our lives.

After grandpa's death, Grandma Helen was left with the sole responsibility of raising not only her own young daughter, but also my sister and me as well, plus running the family farming/ranching/ crop dusting business. At this time, her father, Great Grandpa Zerfas came to live with us for a short period of time to get the business matters under control. Thus, creating the events which construct the second childhood memory [which made itself known to me in a dream].

For the most part my childhood was filled to capacity with virtual happiness and fond memories.

I had three cousins-Kent, Dennis and Staci. We were raised like brothers and sisters. Like most siblings, we shared overnight campouts, building forts, dividing into driveway basketball teams to play 2 on 2, we played football, raced our bicycles, later trading them for mini-bikes, then motorcycles and eventually cars.

In 1969 Grandma Helen remarried. We were exposed to trips to Disneyland on the west coast, as well as trips to the Gulf Coast, Yellowstone National Park, and the St. Louis Arch to mention just a few. This marriage also exposed us

Whatever It Takes

to alcoholism. Grandma's new husband, who we called Bob, drank frequently. Thank goodness he was a "happy drunk". He did his best to make our childhood happy. Among many other gifts, he bought us horses, a motorcycle and a backyard pool complete with a slide. I imagine it was his way to compensate for his drinking problem.

Grandpa George[my mother's dad] also drank too much, but I loved him. I remember, as a young girl, loading the camper for our outings at the lake where we enjoyed fishing and water skiing. Grandpa always brought along his faithful companion-bourbon. The camping trips were still fun. My mother's brothers, Bob and Melvin had also become an important part of our lives. Uncle Bob taught me how to water ski at a young age. Many weekends were spent at the lake until Grandpa George died in 1973 from alcoholism. I have often thought that a broken heart contributed to his death, as he never recovered from my mother's death. He loved his only daughter tremendously and would tell me stories about her. He would even frequently slip [without realizing it] and call me 'Diana'. I would never correct him, I would let him have his moment of reliving happiness. At the age of 10, death was seeming to be a constant occurance. I thought it happened to all families. I thought it was a part of life.

Dayna Gfeller-Mackley

With both of my grandfathers now gone from my life, I began spending much more time with another very special person-my Great Grandpa Bill. He was Grandpa Harold's father. All the kids in our community called him "Grandpa Bill" or "Uncle Bill". Everyday we would go to his big old farmhouse (which was less than 50 yards from the house which I grew up in). He would let us pop corn in a big pan with out a lid! My! What a mess it would make-but he didn't care, because it would also mean more time we would have to spend with him-cleaning up the mess.

Kent, Dennis, Darla and I (and Staci, when she was old enough) spent just about every day playing 'hide and seek' in his big old house and the 'haunted closet' in the basement. He even taught Dennis how to pee over the fence when he was less than three!

In Grandpa Bill's yard, there was a low spot that would fill with water everytime that it rained and form a large mud hole. We would frolick in it and sling mud at each other for hours. When that wasn't fun anymore, Grandpa Bill would line each of us up next to his house and hose us off with cold water from the hydrant. We ran home bawling! So many memories...*almost* all of them fond!

Whatever It Takes

All our friends were always welcome at Grandpa's house too. We'd run into his house and shout "Let's go to town!".

He would load all of us [no matter how many] into his Chevy Impala and take us to the store, buying us whatever candy we wanted. One time, Grandpa even let Dennis [at the mature age of 4] drive while sitting on his lap. Dennis didn't make the turn around the curve and we all had to climb out the passenger side window of the car. I think Gandpa Bill had been drinking too! He was a very big influence in my life until he died in 1976.

The next few years brought a few more cousins-four on my dad's side and four more on my mother's side of the family as well.These years also meant finishing grade school, Jr. high school and then the experience of high school.

Life was good! I loved sports, cheerleading and friends-especially boys. My freshman year, I became aware of a young man who had always been around and had grown up right along with me. His name was Denny and I found him interesting. It didn't take long for me to decide that he was my soul-mate. We dated off and on through out high school. I knew from our first date that this was the guy I wanted to spend the rest of my life with. It did, however, take him a bit longer to figure out my plans included him. On October of my senior year he gave me an engagement ring and asked me to marry him. We planned a May wedding, for the weekend after I'd graduate from high school. I was 18. He was 20. Life was not just good-It was great!!

Three~ Creating Our Life

The day before the wedding, a visit to the doctor revealed that we were going to be parents. We were both extremely happy and Denny couldn't wait to share our news. My life was coming together perfectly. All I ever wanted and dreamed of-a family-was about to happen.

Two weeks after our wedding we were living in the exact same house that my parents left behind the morning that they died. I was keeping busy making our home and fixing up a nursery for the baby that was due to arrive on December 25. Denny was employed driving a truck hauling cattle. When he was away I had plenty of company. My sister lived next door with Grandma Helen, she was a junior in high school at this time, and Kent, Dennis and Staci lived just 2 houses away. We were all still very close and by now Staci [who was 8 years younger than me]and I had formed a bond like none that most sisters are lucky enough to share.

I couldn't wait to become a mother. On Sunday evening, December 27, 1981, while watching tv with Denny, my water broke. Two hours later, our first child-Justin Cole Mackley was born. From the beginning, we called him 'Cole'. He was perfect! Cole filled my days and nights with love and excitement. I had prayed for a strong healthy baby boy for months, and now he was here-right here in my arms where he belonged. He was born on Denny's parents' 25 th wedding anniversary. We had to call them in Hawaii and tell them their first grandson had arrived. They returned home a week later and came to visit. When they held my son in their arms for the first time, I witnessed a look in their eyes. This was the first time I had felt a pain in my heart of being parentless. I realized that I had created a gift for my parents and they were not here to accept that gift. Once again, as always, the rest of my family stepped up to the task they had always accepted. Cole became everyone's baby. Grandma Helen and Bob adored him, Uncle David and Aunt Judy became surrogate grandparents and all my cousins showered him with attention. I didn't think life could get any better. What a blessing!

Life in general was changing daily. Five months later, in May, we were most definitley outgrowing our house. Who would have thought that a baby would aquire so many posessions? In May 1982, we moved to a farm eleven miles from town owned by Denny's great aunt. Denny was no longer driving a truck, but now farming and ranching with his dad and younger brother. The new occupation allowed him much more time at home with me and Cole. We spent

Whatever It Takes

just about every summer weekend at the lake. Denny and I enjoyed skiing and camping and Cole loved playing in the sand and cooling off in the water. We were a happy family.

Summer soon passed and winter blew in. We were snow skiing in Colorado in March 1983 with Denny's sister and her husband. I fainted in the shower and when I opened my eyes all three of them were standing over the bathtub looking at me. A trip to the doctor confirmed what I already knew, but hadn't shared with anyone…our second child was due October 30.

The months flew by and Cole was anxiously awaiting the arrival of his 'be-be'. Denny and I were busy with family and farm life. On the first Monday night in October Denny came in the house and said we had cattle out. Cole and I joined him in the pickup for the rough and bumpy ride through the pasture rounding up cattle. At seven o'clock the next morning Denny left for work and I started having contractions at 7:30. Since this was a time before wireless phone service, I called my mother in law and told her to hurry. We traveled a very exciting trip to the hospital and arrived just in time for the doctor to catch the baby! Fifty minutes of labor!! Not bad! I could make a career of this! Our little girl was born on October 4, 1983. Tasha Diane

Dayna Gfeller-Mackley

Gfeller Mackley was named after my mother. She was beautiful. I watched my mother in law hold this precious life in her arms and once again, I longed for my own parents.

Denny was informed of Tasha's surprise early arrival and he drove to the hospital to meet his new daughter.

I soon discovered that this "baby business" was so easy and rewarding. Motherhood came naturally to me. I didn't mind being pregnant or giving birth-I could, however, do without the sleep deprivation. Unlike Cole, Tasha didn't require alot of sleep. I did.

Also, unlike Cole, Tasha was very inquisitive and at one year old, she was into everything. And she did her demolition silently. To find her, I just followed her trail of messes.

With two children under the age of two, Denny, apparently, didn't think I had enough to do. On Christmas Eve 1983, he brought home a puppy. "Keystone" loved our family and she was so cute-It was too late to say 'no'.

One day during the next spring, I was working outside in the yard and lost track of Cole. I couldn't find him anywhere. With Tasha in tote, I looked for him in the barn, the tree rows, the pens and all the sheds. I was beginning to get scared. Frantically, I was on my way to the house to phone for help when I heard a childish giggle coming from the doghouse. On my hands and knees, I spied him in the back of the big doghouse with Keystone and her 10 puppies. I was so happy to see him I cried. All I could think of was "What would I ever do if something happened to one of these kids?" I could never bear losing one of my children. Snapping myself back to reality, I reminded myself -'Not to worry...that's something you only read about. It would never happen to me.'

In April 1985, we moved back into town, to a bigger house with lots of driveway and sidewalk for Cole and Tasha to ride their tricycles on and lots of neighbor kids for them to play with. This move also carried with it a hefty mortgage payment. In order to make ends meet Denny started hauling cattle again and was on the road a significant amount of time. His new job worked out well for both of us. It demanded longer hours and hard work, but he was happy driving a truck, seeing the country and I was content to stay at home and be a full time mother-the mother that I, myself, had always longed for. I baked cookies, taught the kids to ride bikes, play ball and swim among other things. Occassionally we would pack up and go with Denny in the truck. The kids would like the adventure, but go stir-crazy after time.

In March 1986, I had my annual checkup and got some surprising news. I was pregnant again! Cole and Tasha were so excited and could hardly wait until the end of October to get their new baby. Denny seemed virtually uneffected by the news. Myself...I was a bit concerned about how I was going to take care of three babies, a house, a yard, and a husband who still acted like a child himself most of the time. I love Denny and I love being married, but I'll admit- I liked it when he left on the truck because it was then that I got the kids all to myself and I got to be mom *and* dad. Cole, Tasha, and I had become so very close and I liked that. They had become my soulmates.

My third pregnancy was advancing rapidly and by June, so was my waist size and my weight. Everyone was making fun of my abnormally large abdomen. At my monthly checkup in July, I expressed concerns about my size and weight gain of 60 pounds [which was much greater that my earlier pregnancies]. At five feet seven inches I normally weigh about 110 pounds. I was really uncomfortable, physically and I was finding it very difficult to breathe in any position. My physician brushed it off saying "you're bound to be bigger with your third pregnancy". At my next checkup in late August, I told my doctor that something was wrong. I expressed the possibility of miscalculating my due date. For my peace of mind, my doctor ordered a sonogram for the next day.

I remember so vividly laying on the exam table in the darkened room. The sonogram technician was scanning my abdomen with her equipment. It was only moments later, but seemed longer, when she smiled and said "Well, I'll be...". Immediately I inquired about what she was seeing, but she kept silent, still searching my abdomen with her device. Again I asked her. And again-"What do you see?" I was starting to get alarmed. Then she said it..."there are four arms and four legs." I remember praying silently "please God, let there be two heads!". Then I started to cry. I wondered how I was ever going to manage four children under the age of four all by myself. She suggested a short break so I could gather my emotions and to call Grandma Helen. She had offered to watch Cole and Tasha while I went for my appointment. I needed to let her know that I was going to be longer than I had anticipated since they wanted to study all the new information and make sure that each of the twins were developing normally. I asked Grandma Helen not to share the 'twin news' until I had time to adjust to it myself and to tell Denny. I remember walking around in a daze the rest of the day feeling sorry for myself and almost afraid to go home because it all seemed so unreal. I went shopping and bought Cole and Tasha each a new "surprise" toy because I felt sorry for them as well. They were about to undergo a major change in their lives as well. They were so used to having all my time and attention and now they were going to have to share it with not one, but two new babies. They didn't seem too bothered about the idea. At first I didn't think they understood the term 'twins' until Cole smiled and said "one for me and one for Tash!". It was then that I decided it would all turn out OK. I would do whatever it takes to make sure my family adjusted.

Later that evening when Denny called from a pay phone I announced the twin news to him. He was so excited. He hung up and called all of his buddies to brag. I guess he thought that two babies meant he was twice the man!

After sleeping on the idea of twins, my attitude changed too. I began thinking of the positive aspects of the whole deal. For instance, I reminded myself that there would never be one child left behind when the older ones go to school, as the last two will go together. And four was a good number- it's the number of children we initially agreed that we wanted. The problem wasn't as big as I had made it. In the

Whatever It Takes

next few days I had put together two complete nurseries and had everything ready for two babies instead of one. Now we wait!

As luck would have it, the next weekend Denny was home. We took the time to pick out [and actually agree on] two girls names and two boys names. That very same night, eight days after learning that I was carrying twins, I went into labor at midnight. I called the hospital to inform them of a twin delivery that was coming in and I called Grandma Helen to come to our house to stay with Cole and Tasha while they slept-unaware of what was going on.

At this point labor was progressing rapidly. Staffing at the hospital was inadequate for delivering premature [32 week gestation] twins even though I had called ahead to warn them.The setting was total chaos. Between admission, IV's, Xrays, and very intense contractions Denny disappeared to the hallway. Baby A, Dalton, was born at 4:48 a.m. At least he was crying, that was a good sign which indicated strong healthy lungs. Then things went downhill fast. Doctors were shouting, then whispering, then shouting. No one would answer any questions I was asking. I knew something was wrong but no one was giving any clues to what. I was still having strong contractions and was in alot of pain and no one would stay with me and tell me what was going on. I couldn't breathe. I thought I was dying. Then I remembered... I asked "Where's my other baby?" "Did you forget there were two?"... Still no one would answer me. Then Denny appeared with a worried look on his face. I told him something was wrong. He said they were taking me into surgery, then the doctors asked him to leave.

I remember being wheeled into the operating room and the doctor asking me if I could feel the baby moving. At that point the contractions were one -on -top- of -the -other and so strong that I could feel little else. Amidst all the confusion I was put in a deep sleep.

I awoke, in a fog, to someone pressing hard on my abdomen. I tried to pull their hands away, but couldn't. I slept again. The next time I woke up I could hear voices. My sister in law and my father in law. I heard her tell him that I looked awful and that my skin was almost transparent. I couldn't see them, but I could hear them and I wanted to say "Hello...I can hear you!". I slept again.

The next time I woke up, my doctor was standing at my bedside. I thought he said "we did everything we could—but your baby died." I slept again. When I woke up the next time, I remembered an awful nightmare that I had, but Denny was there so I knew everything was OK. The doctor

Whatever It Takes

was there too. He explained to me that we had a little boy, but that I couldn't see him yet because they transported him to a special care nursery 100 miles away [to be on the safe side] because he was eight weeks early. He gave me a phone number that I could call to check on my baby any hour of the day and keep up with his progress. Then he said it…"The second twin died." He explained that the second twin got hung up in my hips and they couldn't free him. He said "I'm sorry, but at least you still have one baby to take home."

He was right. After all I only found out eight days ago that there were two babies, and I did still have one to take home. So why do I feel so bad?…I slept again.

The next day Denny drove the hundred miles to see our third child, a son, Dalton Keith Gfeller Mackley, in the neonatal intensive care unit. He returned later in the day with pictures of him. He had reddish-blonde hair and he weighed four pounds and two ounces. He looked so skinny, laying naked, in the heated isolette, with tubes and wires hooked up to his fragile little body, but I already loved him.

Turns out that his twin brother, Caton Nick, also weighed four pounds and two ounces and had reddish-blonde hair as well. The funeral director and his wife carried his tiny little casket into my hospital room the day of the funeral service so I could see him. I wasn't able to attend. I had to stay in the hospital for seven days. Denny's parents helped him make the funeral arrangements and my mother in law took Denny shopping to buy a little blue layette set and a soft baby blue blanket- something perfect to lay him to rest in. Two girlfriends came to the hospital to distract me during the service. They meant well, but it didn't distract me. Caton was buried in the plot beside my parents, the one which was reserved for my final resting place when my life ended. This wasn't how life was intended to be-I know it.

After my week in the hosptial, I was still awfully uncomfortable at my incision site where a bandage covered the staples. Denny came to take me home. I desperately missed Cole and Tasha and I needed to see them. They were staying with Grandma Helen part of the time and Aunt Debbie part of the time. After having lunch, Cole, Tasha, Denny and I traveled to see Dalton. He was eight days old and I finally got to hold him in my arms for the first time. I cried. I cried because I was happy and I cried because I was sad-something was missing. I felt that a piece of my heart had been ripped out.

Whatever It Takes

Dalton had to stay in the NBICU until he was strong and healthy enough to go home with us.

Our family {minus Dalton} went home to our house. We went home to two nurseries-with no babies. I felt sick. Life is so fragile. I learned that whatever happens-happens. You can't undo what has been done. I felt so alone on the inside, but carried on as though everything was normal and fine on the outside [for everyone else's peace of mind]. That, my friend, is exhausting! I had made up my mind that I would do whatever it takes to make sure our lives went on as before.

The next day Denny had to go back to work. For me, the next twenty days were spent commuting back and forth from home to the hospital to see Dalton. Finally, on September 28, we got to bring him home with us. At last, we were all under one roof. I still felt a sense of loss. I kept telling myself that surely everyone, in their lifetime, must suffer the loss of a child. If that is so, then I was glad my turn was over with and I had my whole future ahead of me. Afterall, I was only twenty three. And, I assumed that Caton's death made me exempt from ever going through the death of a child again in my lifetime. I had a husband who loves me, three healthy children, a nice home, everything I could want. I reminded myself of these things daily, but it never changed the fact that I didn't feel 'whole', something was missing, clearly absent.

One afternoon Dalton was sleeping in his baby swing. It was going back and forth in sync with the lullaby playing from his favorite music box. At that moment, I thought "I should have two swings, two carseats, 2 cribs, and most of all, two babies". I think this was the first time I really cried and began to heal of Caton's death. It had been almost three months.

Just as with Cole and Tasha, I had formed a special bond with Dalton. Something about him was different. I didn't know if it was because of the circumstances surrounding his birth or if it was because he was "a half of a whole"-being an identical twin. He was just so much more connected to me and needy of my attention. There were times I would look at him and wonder if he could sense the loss of his identical twin and if he longed for his companionship.

Over the next months, Dalton grew and developed at the adjusted rate of 2 months behind most babies his age [which made up the prematurity of his birth]. At least he slept through the night which was a change of pace from the

Whatever It Takes

sleepless nights of Tasha's infant year. He played together so well with Cole and Tasha. He especially bonded with Cole and he adored the big brother who shared his room and packed him around upon his hip.

Before we knew it, a whole year had flown by and Christmas snuck up on us. All three kids were anxious to tear into the wrapping paper and open the gifts Santa had brought. Dalton's eyes were sparkling with excitement that Christmas morning as he played with his new toys.

Two days later was Cole's sixth birthday. I was baking his birthday cake when Dalton woke from his nap. He was a bit fussy and running a low-grade fever. Initially I thought he was teething because his back molars had been trying to come through. As the evening continued, he got fussier, more irritable and was 'clingy' to me. By nine o'clock his fever was 101 degrees and I called our family doctor, who told me to give him childrens' tylenol, push the fluids, and to bring him to the clinic in the morning if he hadn't improved.

Our night was virtually sleepless. Denny went to sleep in the boys' room and I put Dalton into bed with me. The fever and vomitting continued throughout the night. We walked the floors, rocked in the chair, took warm baths....I tried everything and he wouldn't seem to settle down long enough to get comfortable. Early in the morning I showered, then bathed Dalton and woke Denny so we could be at the clinic when it opened.

The morning air was blowing snow and bitter cold, but we made it to the clinic just as they were opening so we were the first in line to see the doctor.

Immediately the situation spiralled downward. {I often have wondered what I would have done if we would have still been at our home-30 minutes from the hospital, and had we not been in the company of a good physician.}

Upon the arrival at the clinic Dalton began experiencing severe seizures. What I was witnessing was so frightening and it was out of my control. I don't deal with things well when they are out of my control. Most of all, I don't like the helpless feeling of being out of control.

Denny, Dalton, and myself accompanied the doctor to the emergency room. In the cold, white, sterile room the doctor tried without success to start an IV medication to hault the seizures. They poked him in the arms, the legs, and even made a bloody mess of his neck trying unsuccessfully to get the IV started in his jugular vein. Resorting to a rectal catheter, they were finally able to stabilize him. The next thing I recall is Dalton and I (and the doctor and two

Whatever It Takes

EMT's) in an ambulance enroute to an advanced level hospital 100 miles away. Denny followed closely behind in our 4-wheel drive pickup. While on the way to the hospital, the doctor was suggesting that he possibly could have contracted spinal meningitis, but it couldn't be confirmed until his spinal fluid was tested. Upon arrival in the pediatric ICU a spinal tap came back "negative". The doctors were back to square one and began running other tests, still unable to identify the source of my childs' illness. Dalton's health was deteriorating rapidly. His organs were failing one by one, his lungs were filling with fluid and he was slipping in and out of a coma. Around 4:30 pm his heart and respirations ceased. A team of doctors and nurses revived him and he was put on a ventilator. An air-ambulance was called and I flew with Dalton and a team of flight nurses to yet another acute care facility. The plane had not yet reached flight altitude when Dalton's heart stopped beating for the second time. CPR was administered the entire 30 minutes of flight and the flight nurses were on the phone with hospital physicians, who were constantly dictating orders to try another drug. I had never been so scared in my life. My child was dying and I could do nothing to help him. The flight nurses wouldn't let me unbuckle my seat belt and come to Dalton's side. I just wanted to let him know that I was with him-that I hadn't abandoned him. I thought that if he could just hear my voice his heart would beat again. The flight nurses paid no attention to my insistant pleading and ordered me to stay in my seat. I sat silently and resorted to prayer. I wondered why God would listen to me now, only calling on him when I was in most desperate need. I also questioned him— What could I have done to make him punish me so harshly, to hurt me by taking another of my children? I questioned why a loving God would make a toddler suffer such an illness. Dalton had never done anything bad-to anyone-nothing to deserve what was being done to him now.

I knew we were in very serious trouble when a helicopter was waiting at the airport to transport my sick baby to the roof of the hospital. No one would give me any answers to the questions I was asking.

Where was God now, when I really needed his help?

After arrival at the hospital the doctors tried repeatedly to restore life to Dalton's no longer beating heart. At this point I envisioned my twins having a brief conversation: Caton saying "Dalton, I miss you! Come to me, I need you!" And Dalton answering "I miss you too Caton, I want to play, but mommy will cry if I leave her..." Dalton died 5

Whatever It Takes

minutes after arriving in the ICU. "Time of death 7:05 pm 12-27-87". I will never forget those words.

I was numb. Yet I was horrified, I was angry-I wanted to hit someone, anyone, I was hurt. What would I ever tell Denny? He and his parents were still enroute to the hospital, probably 2 hours away.

I asked everyone to leave the intensive care unit and leave me alone with my child. The doctor unhooked the life support system so I could pick Dalton up and hold him in my arms. I rocked him, knowing I would never hold his warm body to mine again. I recall this as being one of the most peaceful times in my life. Looking back, I know there must have been an angel in my presence in that room.

Denny arrived 2 hours later. I was still rocking Dalton. His body was cold and still. His little fingers were stiffly wrapped around mine. After ten o'clock 2 men came to take my baby's body away. It broke my heart to have them lift him from my arms, having to pry away his fingers that had formed around mine. My arms had never felt so empty-ever. We checked into a hotel near the hospital. Our life with Dalton had ended. We needed to call my family back home. They were caring for Cole and Tasha. Someone had to tell them their brother had died.

Dayna Gfeller-Mackley

We started our silent journey home the next morning, only stopping for lunch and to buy Denny a new suit for the funeral. In my possession, I had the clothes Dalton was dressed in when we left our home 24 hours earlier... a blue sweatsuit adorned with teddy bears that he had gotten for Christmas only days ago, and his "blankie" (a handmade quilt with elephants on the flannel backing). The sweatsuit and the quilt still held the baby scent of my innocent 15 1/2 month old little boy with big, sparkling brown eyes framed with long eyelashes.

What had went wrong? Two days earlier he was perfectly healthy, squealing with delight as he tore the wrapping paper off his Christmas gifts. The doctors were unable to diagnose the illness and an autopsy was requested.

As we entered our driveway at home everything looked normal-much the same as every other time we had arrived home. But it wasn't the same, things were desperately different now.

I wandered into the boys' room. Cole's bed was still unmade as we had left in a hurry when Dalton was sick. Dalton's crib was empty with the exception of his favorite brown bear with the red bow. It, too, still smelled of his baby hands that had previously hugged the plush bear.

Whatever It Takes

Our next stop was Uncle David's house where Cole and Tasha would be waiting. I wanted to hold them both in my arms again and tell them I love them. Many relatives had gathered there and our small community was carrying in dishes of food, just as always when someone dies. When I laid my eyes on Cole and Tasha, I could no longer contain my emotions. We cried together. Both of my grandmothers were crying too. They knew how I felt. Twenty two years earlier their children, my parents, also were taken at a young age. Not as young as Dalton-but still, too young. I had never before looked at my grandmothers in that "light" before-as grieving parents. After eating a meal that had been prepared for our family, we went home. Just the four of us, no longer five. I bathed Cole and Tasha, dressed them for bed and tucked them in .

Still not knowing what had caused Dalton's illness, I decided to clean the house and to disinfect everything. If it was a germ that had started this nightmare, I was going to end it before it did any more damage. I was so tired when I finished, but I still couldn't sleep. The next couple of days were spent picking out burial clothes, a casket, music and flowers. I wondered who thought of this whole process [the funeral business] and WHY? I guess it's *finality* [if that's a word]. It's closure- a license to move on.

As the casket bearers carried Dalton's casket down the aisle to exit the sactuary to the waiting hearse outside, they passed Cole standing by Denny and I . He lifted his small 6 year old hand, waved, and whispered "bye Dalton".

He had accepted the loss and let go, why couldn't I?

The weeks to follow were lonely. My arms which had always before carried Dalton, were now empty. Both of Denny's brothers had a baby the same age as Dalton. I often wondered if they knew how fortunate they were to still have their babies. It took me a long time before I even wanted to be in the same company of their babies or hold them. There were even times when I would ask God a very selfish question…'why not one of their babies, why mine?'. I would never want one of my nieces or nephews to die, but I didn't want my baby to die either.

I regularly, visited the graves of my twins at the cemetery, decorating the small mounds with flowers and toys. I told myself they were happy-at least they were together, as identical twins should be.

Eleven weeks after Dalton's death I got a call from our family physician. He asked me to come to his office. The autopsy results were in and he would explain everything to me in words I could understand. He read down the list laying in front of him. I heard him tell me how each

Whatever It Takes

individual organ had been removed from Dalton's body, weighed and examined only to reveal that each one had failed and deteriorated over a 24 hour period. He taught me about the rare disease that took over Dalton's small body-Reyes Syndrome: a disease that is linked to flu and chicken pox and use of asprin. I couldn't, wouldn't understand. Dalton hadn't been sick. No flu, no chickenpox, not even a cold. He had certainly never been given asprin in his short life. The doctor went on to explain in detail the pain and devastation that my child had experienced in his last hours of life. With painful reality, I now understood why he was so fussy and irritable the night before we went to the doctor- due to infection, his little brain had swelled beyond the limits of his skull causing the headache which lead to the seizures, coma, then death. This was such an ugly disease. I couldn't fathom how it found it's place in our home, within one of my children. The need to find research about Reyes Syndrome led to very little information about the disease. What little information I did locate seemed to point to death being the most humane outcome of the possibilities.

The months to follow would take alot of support from my family and close friends. I joined a support group of parents experienced with the death of a child. I found myself in situations not wanting to let Cole and Tasha out of my sight for fear of them being taken from me too. Any time they complained of not feeling well or anytime they spiked a temperature I panicked and rushed them to the doctor.

Our lives in general were changed whether we wanted change or not. Denny was spending alot of time away from home, still hauling cattle. Business had really picked up which kept him busy, but didn't keep his mind off of everything that had happened. Hauling cattle is a hard and grueling lifestyle but it allowed us the income needed to pay our soaring medical bills. More loads meant more income, but also less sleep. I could see that Denny was struggling, and that drugs were becoming a necessity to keep him awake the absurd hours he was working. At the same time, [the drugs] were an escape from all the pain and confusion in our lives. Drugs were becoming a crutch which held him up.

For me, my friends became my support system. Especially my best friend, Shirley. She had children the same ages as ours, her youngest being only 2 weeks older than Dalton. We enjoyed each others company while our kids played. She listened compassionatly while I talked and I listened while she shared her fears. She had recently been diagnosed with cancer and it was spreading quickly. I cared

Whatever It Takes

for her 3 boys while she and her husband searched doctors and clinics for healing and treatment. With her, I was able to focus on something besides my own loss. For months I witnessed as she slowly, was losing her own children, but in a different way-she would be departing this life and would be leaving them behind. We talked on the phone everyday that we weren't together. She became my source of strength, my hero.

By August 1988, I was spending alot of time in the truck with Denny during the fall cattle run (our busiest time of year) . At my bi-annual physical required to drive a truck, my doctor discovered my fourth pregnancy. Denny and I were surprised but very excited. Cole and Tasha were very happy to hear that they would be sharing a new brother or sister as well. A new baby would never replace Dalton, but we hoped it would fill a vacancy that his death created in our hearts. We decided not to tell anyone until Thanksgiving. No one except Shirley. I thought my good news would help cheer her up.

I had spent a week with Denny and when we got home I drove to her house to share my news about the pregnancy.

She was resting on the sofa when I entered and I wasn't prepared for what I saw. After a week away from her, she had changed drastically. She was so frail and sick, losing her battle with cancer. All I could do was hold her hand-unable to tell her my good news, about how happy I was, when she was so ill.

I was aware that she didn't have much time left and I so desperately wanted to ask her to check in on my boys when she got to heaven, to give them hugs and kisses from me and tell them I missed them. But I couldn't. She died two days later. I helped her husband pick out the clothes that she would be buried in and I told him about the day I came to tell her I was pregnant. He smiled and said "she knew you were pregnant and she knew why you didn't tell her". They buried Shirley on her youngest son's second birthday. I hope she knows what an inspiration she was to me. She allowed me to see that no matter how tough you think your life is, no matter how challenging it may be for you-There is someone, somewhere that is worse off than yourself. I will always remember her and the gift of friendship she gave me.

My pregancy was progressing normally with four and a half months to go. Right after Thanksgiving, I got up during the night to go to the bathroom only to discover that I was bleeding. I called my ob/gyn at home and he advised that I come to see him in the morning. I wasn't having contractions, but I was dilating prematurely. He sent me home with medication and orders for strict bedrest for the remaining 4 months of my pregancy.

Denny and I returned home expecting a long, slow pregnancy to follow. Four days later I went into labor. I was admitted to the hospital and many heroic measures were taken to deliver a 24 week gestation infant. I was given medication to delay labor (even a few days) trying to "buy" some time. Drugs were used to rapidly develop the baby's premature lungs. By late that evening delivery could no longer be delayed. Jesse Dayne was born at 9:37 pm on December 9, 1988 weighing 1 pound and ten ounces. He resembled Tasha almost identically with his reddish blonde hair and long eyelashes. He had the most perfect little fingernails at the end of each of his long slender fingers. However, his lungs were not perfectly formed and held no chances of viability. Denny and I were allowed to hold Jesse wrapped in his soft blue blanket and tiny hat for three hours until his little heart ceased to beat any longer. Mysteriously, once again, I experienced a very peaceful feeling while holding my dying child. The funeral home was contacted and Denny and I returned home the next day, alone. We were forced to go shopping to buy a baby doll, borrowing it's little blue sleeper and matching hat to use as burial clothes. We planned and attended another funeral for yet another of our precious children, and bought another headstone to mark yet another grave in our family burial plot…Something I decided I could never, ever go through again, ever.

Life at home was slowly returning to normal (whatever normal happens to be) other than the fact that I was feeling emotionally exhausted. I was becoming quite convincing- living as though nothing effected me. At my six week check up with my OB/GYN, we discussed my physical and emotional well being. My doctor was concerned about my emotional stability after years of scarring. He worried that things were eventually going to build up inside me and need to escape. Once again I told him that I could handle it-no need to worry. I would do whatever it takes.

However, I still felt the overwhelming presence of the need to have another baby. I assumed that my chances of giving birth to any more children had expired with Jesse, but I wasn't ready to give up just yet.

My doctor informed me of a medical procedure that could possibly allow me to carry to term. We talked extensively of this and I shared my thoughts as well. I

Whatever It Takes

wasn't [as a mother or a woman] ready to stop having children yet. I returned home to share the news about the possibility of conceiving again with Denny. He was relieved to finally hear my thoughts as well, as I hadn't willingly talked about the loss to anyone.

Life continued to move forward. I was discouraged, but at the same time I was hopeful that we may [once again] heal and our lives could eventually feel "whole" .

By the end of April 1989, a home pregnany test confirmed my suspicions. I was a bit scared, but so happy. I scheduled an appointment, reluctant to share the news with anyone yet. Blood tests, sonograms and frequent visits for special care / high risk prenatal treatment reassured me that everything was progressing normally. At 16 weeks surgery was required to stitch my cervix to hopefully prevent premature dialation. My due date was estimated at December 15. Within four months, the pregnancy was difficult to conceal and we began telling others of our expected arrival.

I vividly remember saying "If you can't be supportive and say something nice-don't say anything at all." Some said nothing, many were supportive but questioned why we would put ourselves in a position to experience another loss. No one could understand our feelings. Not unless they had also experienced and shared our feelings of loss...the loss of a child. I guess you could say we were trying to create our own happiness.

The pregnancy was closely monitored by a high risk specialist and my activities were limited to practically nothing. That was the hardest part for me because I have never been the kind of person who can relax and sit idle very long at a time.

In August, Cole started second grade and Tasha began kindergarten which was on Monday, Wednesday and Friday. Having both kids in school allowed me plenty of time to relax with my feet up and Denny and the kids both helped out around the house.

By the first of November I felt I had accomplished a major milestone when I began experiencing mild, irregular contractions. Quite sure that I wouldn't make it to my December due date I began preparing for the arrival of our new little one.

At my weekly regular check up on November 13 the doctor witnessed the regular [and getting stronger] contractions. I told him that I'd been tollerating them for about two weeks. From experience, I knew that each day I carried the baby in my womb -the stronger it would be. A sonogram and a thorough examination revealed that the

Whatever It Takes

baby weighed approximately six pounds. At 36 weeks gestation, the doctor told me that the baby was strong enough to deliver whenever I decided the contractions were getting too uncomfortable to continue.

Denny was loading cattle in Oregon and I didn't want him to miss the birth so I decided I could wait one more day. On Tuesday morning, November 14, I got Cole off to school and got Tasha and myself ready to take my grandma Christmas shopping as I had promised. I didn't tell my grandma that I was having contractions. They were getting stronger, but I could still conceal them. We drove the 30 miles to town and spent the morning gathering all her Christmas presents for everyone. I would disappear behind a clothes rack everytime I felt the need to do my 'deep-cleansing' breathing. She wasn't aware that I was in labor until we stopped for lunch on the way home. Normally, I have a big appetite. But, after several trips to the restroom and I had barely touched my food, she started asking questions. She suggested that I looked very uncomfortable and that I was quite pale. I confessed-"I've been having contractions for two weeks and I'm going to have this baby today, as soon as Denny gets home."

Needless to say, we went straight home. She helped me pack and get Cole and Tasha bathed and dressed. We had the car all loaded when Denny arrived home. As soon as he showered, we were on our way.

The hospital was one hundred miles away. Half way there I realized that I hadn't eaten much and I was hungry. I knew I would be getting nothing but ice chips and IV fluids once we arrived at the hospital, so I made Denny stop at a Dairy Queen for a burger, fries and a chocolate milk shake. Now I was ready to have a baby!

We arrived at the hospital around 5 pm. I was admitted and set up in a birthing room. There was just one problem: My doctor had nine babies waiting to be born (including mine and a set of twins)! Since I was the only one who had stitches securely closing my cervix, I would be held till last, if possible- Lucky Me!

Denny, Cole and Tasha passed the time watching the fetal monitor and visiting with the nurses, all which had fallen in love with 'adorable' Cole and 'beautiful' Tasha. Did you know that *Dominoes Pizza* will deliver to the birthing room? {Yes Denny and the kids ordered pizza! The three of them and my doctor ate pizza in front of me!}

At 9:30 the doctor made the decision to remove the stitches in my cervix. All the babies had been delivered

Whatever It Takes

except mine and the twins {who were progressing slowly}. I quickly dialated to ten and a healthy baby girl was delivered at 10:10 pm.

Jenna Nicole was screaming in the background when we called home to let everyone know that she had arrived safe and healthy weighing 5 pounds and 15 ounces. Cole and Tasha were immediately impressed with their new baby sister and forgot I was even in the room as they hovered over her bassinet. I finally got to hold Jenna after "Daddy" and both siblings had their turns.

What a wonderful moment! All five of us sitting in my hospital bed fussing over this new life God had blessed us with. Finally, I was happier than I had been in a long while. Two days later we were all at home… together.

A baby and two children in school was keeping me plenty busy. Time was flying by quickly and life was perfect. School was soon out for the summer. The kids and I would take trips with Denny in the truck. Cole and Tasha loved to swim so I'd take all three of the kids to the pool every week. I loved to watch them laugh and be happy. Who could ask for more? A loving husband, healthy happy children, nice home, great friends and wonderful family….I had it all….but I always, always yearned for what was missing.

A couple of months after Jenna's first birthday I was watching her follow Cole and Tasha while they played. She looked like a fifth wheel on a car. She always tried to be a part of whatever game they were playing and tried to participate in everything they were doing. Because of her age, she didn't fit in, or more appropriately-wasn't allowed to fit in. Tasha was six years older than Jenna and Cole was eight years older. The two older siblings shared a very special, close-knit bond and it didn't include Jenna.

Now that Jenna was walking [running actually], feeding herself, talking and becoming more independent daily, I felt the need for another baby. One for Jenna to share the bond with that Cole and Tasha had. I shared my feelings with Denny. I told him I wanted to have <u>one</u> more child. After all, four was a good number- two older children and two younger children would complete our family.

October 1991~ I was well into my second month of my first trimester. I felt great! Lots of energy and no morning sickness. A sonogram and extensive tests revealed a healthy baby due at the end of May. Once again, surgery would be necessary at sixteen weeks and another sonogram at twenty weeks.

In mid December I came down with the flu and a severe cold with a bad cough. I was very sick and became extremely tired and run down. For days I ran a high fever and coughed uncontrollably. My symptoms gradually improved except for the cough. By the end of January, I began experiencing some mild, irregular contractions. My doctor prescribed medications to stop the contractions and advised me to take it easy-limiting my activities to practically nothing. During the month of February the contractions persisted mild and irregular.

On March 2, I was resting on the sofa with my feet elevated on a pillow. The kids were playing and watching TV when I felt a bit of fluid leak. This continued through out the evening. Denny got home at midnight and I informed him of what was happening. By four A.M. I was spotting and my contractions were strong, regular and 5 minutes apart.I was too uncomfortable to sleep so I rose with intentions of letting Denny sleep a couple of more hours while I showered and packed for our trip to the hospital. At six o'clock I had everything ready to go and a bag packed for Cole, Tasha and Jenna. I phoned Uncle

David and Aunt Judy and explained what was going on and made plans to leave the children in their care.

Two hours later we were in the emergency room at Hays and the doctor discovered that the stitches in my cervix had tore loose and the amniotic fluid tested positive for an infection. A decision was made to transport me by Life-Flight to Wichita KS for the delivery of our 28-week gestation daughter.

Once again, things were happening so quickly. In my mind, my conscience could hear everyone saying "I told you so..." and "you just had to have another baby-why put yourself through this again?" I was scared and felt so alone. The flight seemed to take forever and Denny wouldn't catch up with me for at least three hours, as he was driving in our car instead of flying.

Once we were at the acute care hospital, more tests were ran. I had never seen so many doctors and nurses...all for one little baby and me. Our little girl [and I mean little!] was born on Tuesday, March 3, 1992 and 5:37 P.M. She wasn't pretty- she was bruised and blue from the neck up. And she wasn't crying. She tried, but only made the sound of a new baby kitten trying to 'meow'. The neonatologist {doctor for sick, high-risk babies} rated her as a 2 on the

Whatever It Takes

APGAR scale at one minute after birth. Her five minute APGAR had improved to 6 (10 being perfectly healthy). She had improved a small bit. I prayed she would improve alot. She weighed 2 pounds and 5 ounces and measured 14 inches in length. I couldn't believe that I had just had a baby-she wasn't due for three months. I was taken to recovery and Denny arrived with in minutes. Three hours later we got to see her in the newborn critical care unit.

Throughout my pregnancy I was so sure that the baby was going to be a boy that I had told Denny he could name the baby if it was a girl. This tiny little human being was so dainty. I thought she needed a dainty name as well. Her dad wanted to name her Laramie. LARAMIE? A 'Laramie' needed a pair of pink cowboy boots and a big ten gallon hat to match. This tiny little creature certainly didn't look like a 'Laramie'. After two days our little girl still had no name. Her neonatologist joked about our 'baby naming situation' adding that he thought she looked like a 'Tori'. Hmmm....Denny and I looked at each other and agreed...Tori it would be! I did let him pick her middle name.

Tori Lynn had a very, very, very long, hard recovery ahead of her. On the third day after Tori was born Denny and I needed to go home and take care of everything that we had left in such a hurry the morning she was born, especially Cole, Tasha, and Jenna. We were given a special '800' number we could call 24 hours a day to check on Tori's progress and status. I called several times a day.

The next several weeks would become an emotional roller coaster ride. On my second day at home I got a call from her doctor saying blood work had detected an infection in the brain causing seizures and she was in very critical condition. I packed my bags, made arrangements for the children and headed to Wichita. Denny was hauling cattle and I would leave a message for him to reach me at the hospital.

When I arrived at the hospital in Wichita it was ten PM and visiting hours were over. The nurses were very kind and understanding. They knew how far I had driven and they let me sneak in to peak at my sick baby before retiring to my hotel room. The next morning I got lost in traffic going to the hospital and was late for the 8 A.M. visiting period. I would have to wait until noon to see her. On my way to see her at noon, an intern intercepted me and in an uncaring monotone told me that a CT scan revealed that my baby's brain had quit growing. He said Tori would most likely die or at best- live to be severly handicapped. Either way, the

Whatever It Takes

outlook was hopeless. He turned his back and walked away. I felt like I had been kicked in the stomach. In a daze, I walked to the parking garage, sat in my car and cried. I cried, then, I prayed. I asked God to fix this mess that my life had become. If He would just heal my baby and make her well, I would do anything . I would do whatever it takes to make it up to Him. I went to the rest of the visiting hours that day knowing I probably had little time to spend with my daughter if she was going to die. I sat at her bedside and talked to her. I wasn't allowed to hold her, it was too painful for her to be carressed because her premature skin was so sensitive to touch. I told her about her family and shared my thoughts with her and I silently prayed for a miracle. I prayed for all the things I thought I needed to pray for, hoping my prayers would be answered. Denny called around midnight to check on her. I couldn't tell him the dreadful news. He sensed the tone of my voice and kept asking if something was wrong. I only told him that I'd had a bad day. I wasn't lying, I just didn't tell him everything. I had made up my mind that I wouldn't tell any one what I knew.

Planning ahead, I figured that all babies just lay around and sleep during their early ages. If she lived, I wouldn't have to explain anything until she couldn't sit up, or crawl or walk. Then I would explain what I had to, when I had to. I didn't want any one to know she was different- not just yet. I knew that her daddy couldn't handle the situation. He was dealing with struggles of his own and didn't even realize it. To protect Tori- this would be our secret for now.

Upon arrival at the hospital the next morning, Tori's neonatologist (special-care infant doctor) was waiting for me at the door. He took me by the arm and said we needed to talk in his office. I informed him that the intern had already told me that Tori was going to die, or at best, be severely handicapped. He replied, "That's what we need to talk about."

He went on to explain that the intern viewed a tiny, tiny, brain on her CT scan, which is what was in my daughter's tiny, tiny head, and he would be diciplined for sharing that information with me. He also went on to say that Tori had adequate blood flow to the brain, as well as good reflexes, and everything was consistant with her size and weight, *but* she was still critical. I didn't believe him and I requested follow-up CT scans, regularly, to prove what he was saying.

I was so happy to see Tori in the unit that day. I desperately wanted to hold her and to feel her. Instead, I sat by her bed and again…I prayed. This time I thanked God.

Whatever It Takes

He does perform miracles. He does answer prayers. The next day I was to return home again.

After spending a day at home, I returned to Wichita. This time with Denny and with Cole, Tasha and Jenna. It was time for them to meet their new baby sister in person, instead of viewing the pictures that I brought home after each visit. We spent three days at the hospital as a family unit before returning home again.

I was well aware that our life was going to be very inconvenient for the next couple of months with me traveling between Wichita and our home, but I would do whatever it takes to get our family together under one roof.

Once again, a late night phone call took me back to Tori's bedside. At a weight of one pound and fifteen ounces, she would need a delicate heart surgery. I located Denny and he arrived the next morning. Tori was scheduled for PDA surgery. A vessel around her heart would need to be surgically closed in order for her to thrive and grow. We were both allowed to hold her momentarilly before surgery. She was seventeen days old when I first held my youngest child-wires, tubes, needles and all!

Dayna Gfeller-Mackley

We waited patiently for hours until the doctor informed us that the surgery was successful. One more hurdle behind us. She was heavily sedated when we went to see her to say good bye before we traveled back home again.

It was proving to be more difficult each time I had to leave her at the hospital and go home to my family. This wasn't going to be easy-getting everyone under one roof, all-the-while keeping my sanity. But I would do it. Three days at home, three days at Wichita. That's pretty much how I lived for the next several weeks. Day by day, Tori was gaining an ounce, sometimes two a day. Her ventilator pressure was decreased each day until eventually she graduated to a C-PAP unit, then supplemental oxygen only. She finished rounds of anibiotics. Needles and tubes began to diminish until she was left only with two IV's, heart and breathing monitors, and seizure medication. Consultations with her doctors and nurses began turning to the possibility of transferring her to a hospital closer to home.

On April 16, she was transported to Hays KS to a special care unit. Now her main goals were to gain weight, bottle feed every three hours and maintain body temperature outside the heated isolette that had been her home since birth. This move allowed me to spend time with her every day and to be with Cole, Tasha, and Jenna everyday as well,

Whatever It Takes

since Hays was only a two hour drive from our home, as opposed to five hours in a car to reach Wichita.

It was happening! We were actually adjusting to another of lifes' difficult situations and the changes that came with it.

As my birthday approached at the end of April, I was able to see a faint light at the end of the tunnel. I really was going to bring this small miracle home to our family one day soon. The tentative date was set for May 8. But first, I would be required to take special care classes in life support and learn to manage the life support system that would accompany us home, as well as spend two nights at the hospital to 'prove ' that I was reliable to care for Tori's special needs.

Finally! The day I had been praying for had arrived. Throughout the final steps of discharging Tori from the hospital, the doctors warned me about all of the draw backs of raising a "special needs" baby such as Tori. On this day Tori was 66 days old. Her brain CT scans were loaded with abnormal peaks indicating damage from bleeding. Hopefully, the damage would repair itself. Tests done on her eyes revealed scar tissue indicating where development of sight would most likely discontinue. Her vision would never be good. Her lungs presented a concern as well. Being on a ventilator for an extended period of time had done damage to them. Her specialist warned me that she would be prone to serious respiratory infections—-all infections, for that matter, as her immune system would have to be built up. I listened to all their discouraging words as they described what kind of life Tori would most likely endure. After all, they had seen it many times before in other infants just like Tori. Most babies born as early as Tori have substantial mental and physical handicaps. Many follow-up visits would be essential for the first two years of her life.

Smiling doctors and nurses lined the corridor as we walked out of the hospital that day. Knowing the future [with Tori] was going to be a challenge, I held my head high, confident that God would never burden me with more than what He knew I could handle. *I Corinthians 10:13 No trial has overtaken you that is not common to man. God is faithful and He will not let you be tested beyond your strength. God will provide the way of escape, that you may be able to endure it.*

Tori joined our family at home on Friday May 8, 1992. She weighed five and one half pounds. It was a big milestone: finally having everyone under one roof! All had adjusted well. The children were growing and thriving, especially Tori. As suggested, we followed up with CT

Whatever It Takes

scans and eye exams every three months. Each visit to the specialists proved to be encouraging. At Tori's 'one year ' exam, there was absolutely no abnormality present on her CT scan, and miraculously, her eye development continued normally—-up and over the scar tissue. Her vision tested perfect!...Just one more miracle performed by God. At her 18 month evaluation, Tori overwhelmed the doctors by passing both- the mental and physical evaluations- with flying colors!!! They told us not to bother bringing her back, that she no longer needed their services.

It was such a relief to have life going so smoothly. And for something unusual——nothing major occurred, just a few ear aches, sore throats, a broken bone or two, and alot of scraped knees...the normal stuff that all families get to experience as part of growing up.

In the midst of 1993, I was becoming quite aware that I had one more major task that I needed to deal with if my "happy" family was going to have a chance of survival.

Over the past seven years of many trials in our life, Denny's addiction to drugs that started out with over-the-counter 'no-doze', had increasingly escalated to incredible amounts of illegal substances. For years, I had known that I needed to intervene, but it was the one confrontation that I was terrified of.

On July 3, 1993, after days of secretly researching drug addiction and treatment facilities, I made a brave decision. I phoned a treatment center and layed out my game plan. I marched into our bedroom, woke Denny and presented him with an ultimatum: The family or the drugs….One of us is leaving…today!

Within two hours we were packed and once again, traveling to Wichita where Denny checked himself into a rehabilitation center for treatment.

For the next thirty days I relocated our family to Wichita in order to do whatever it takes to keep our family from becoming another statistic.

Our families, both mine and Denny's, as well as our 'true' friends became a great support system. We have come to find out that these are the times when you discover just who are <u>really </u>your friends and those who are <u>really not</u>.

Denny attended therapy sessions, awareness classes and lots of N/A meetings. I observed, and daily I could see the "old Denny" slowly emerging. The man I fell in love with and vowed to share the rest of my life with was slowly returning.

Whatever It Takes

We were slowly overcoming another trial in our life. On August 3, thirty days after leaving our home, our family returned-still intact. I thanked God, sure that this would be the last time my faith would be tested. After all, what else could possibly happen?

Denny retired from truck driving and began farming and ranching. He was home every night now, which I liked better, but it required alot more of my time also. Denny and the kids kept my schedule packed.

Our lives seemed to get busier and busier as the children grew older. Cole and Tasha were both involved in sports and eventually the day arrived when the last little one, Tori, started school. I always had the impression that this is when I would finally get a break, I would finally be able to go back to school myself. WRONG!

Between football games, volleyball matches, basketball, trackmeets, cheerleading practice and girl scout events, I was slowly giving up my lifes' passions to be available for everything the kids had going on in their lives'. And the sad thing is…I didn't mind one little bit! I loved being involved in all they had going on. I was experiencing true happiness at this point in my life.

Dayna Gfeller-Mackley

Happiness, however is not to last forever~Tragedy would once again bring all the feelings of uncertaintly to the surface. In 1995, on a dark November morning, a phone call brought back all those unsettling feelings and unanswered questions of death. My uncle from Denver had been killed in a hunting accident in the mountains. In a place where he had always found peace and serenity, he had been shot in the chest.

Throughout my childhood and my adult life, Uncle Bob and I had always had a special relationship. Especially within the last ten years, we had become very close. We had just spent over an hour talking on the phone the evening before he left on this disastrous hunting trip with friends. We made plans for Thanksgiving. In this particular phone call, he shared with me many things [he said] he thought I needed to know. Looking back now, I realize that God allowed this perfect hour of sharing between me and Uncle Bob, as it would be our last conversation. Thank you God for this gift.

At thirty three years of age and with thirty three years of lifes' experiences under my belt, a pattern was becoming quite apparent to me. I am finding that just when I get "comfortable" with my life-something happens to 'shake things up' and to remind me that nothing is forever-except eternity. Certainly, life as we know it, is not forever.

An early morning phone call in July 1997, confirms that. My Aunt phoned me from a hospital thirty miles from home. Her son, my God son, had been in a serious car accident. She went on to add "It's bad." I rushed to the trauma room to see him before they air-lifted him to a critical care facility in Denver. I knew that his life at this point was fragile. His injuries were critical: a punctured lung, broken bones, and a severe brain injury. I returned home to make arrangements for my children and to pack. Denny and I spent the next six days in Denver, where I waited at TJ's bedside for a change in his status. He was comotose and his brain pressure and other vital signs were anything but good. We returned home. It was days before he came out of the coma, and when he did the person he once was, seemed to have gotten lost in behind the blue eyes that once revealed his zest for life.

I will never forget an entry my oldest daughter, Tasha, penned in her journal at this time…"God, please let TJ be OK, don't let him die, I'd miss him too much". I was happy to know that at least she still had faith in God, even after everything that our family had experienced.

Dayna Gfeller-Mackley

The next several weeks were spent traveling from Winona to Denver. We were finally able to see that most of TJ would be returning home someday. Lots of physical and occupational therapy would be required, but we would keep him! He was able to return home in October, continuing therapy for months until he was almost as good as new, except for some memory loss and a slight personality change. I am so thankful that my God son is still alive.

Returning back to our ordinary, but never uneventful life, I was soon caught up in the hurried pace of high school sports, jr. high school sports, school events, cheerleading practices, boyfriend problems, girl friend crisis, little girl emergencies, birthday parties, sleep overs.... You name it! At our house...it's going on! I found out that being a mother is a full time job, but very rewarding. I wouldn't change a thing about my life!

Another year passed~ 1998 rolled in and before I had realized it, school was out for the summer, summer ended, and the fall semester at school began.

Cole was beginning his junior year, which meant a lot more work for me. Tasha, as a freshman, was excited about beginning high school. Jenna was promoted to third grade

Whatever It Takes

and Tori, now a full time student in first grade, was quite the socialite in school.

Tasha made varsity starter on the volleyball team, so Tuesdays and most Saturdays were set aside for attending her games. Cole, an offensive and defensive starter on the high school football squad got all of our attention on Friday nights.

At the end of September, with a 4 - 0 win /loss record, a football injury ended his season, and mine.

With in two weeks he was depressed and came to me with the idea of quitting school. His thoughts were: if he couldn't participate in sports, he didn't want to go to school.

Once again—-another problem. A small problem in scale to what usually arrived in our lives, but still, a problem. After spending an afternoon on the phone, I came up with a solution that both, Cole and I, could live with and agree to. Cole needed very few credits to graduate from high school. An alternative school allowed him to go to school only to get the required classes to graduate, while still working a full-time job. Plus he would graduate a year ahead of schedule. He went to school on Wednesdays, did homework in the evenings, spent weekends with his girlfriend and had a good job. With out all the extra-curricular activities involved with 'normal' high school, his grade point average improved and I got to spend alot more time with him as well {which would later, in the months to come, be an absolute necessity to my own personal survival}.

After a successful volleyball season ended, I looked forward to every single basketball game. Tasha was a varsity starter on the basketball team as well. I took great pride in watching her and her team-mates win with pride and lose (a few) with dignity. I was aware of her athletic talent and looked forward to her high school career with much anticipation. After basketball season, Tasha excelled in the track and field sports as well. She {and I} set some personal goals for her early in the season. As a long jumper, she strived to break the long standing long jump record of sixteen feet and two inches. She also hoped to qualify for the state meet in Wichita at the end of the season.

She met both of those goals! She made the state track and field honor roll [something she was very proud of]. She set a new school record in long jump at seventeen feet - four and one-half inches. She also set records in two relay events with other team mates. At the regional meet, she placed third in the long jump which rewarded her with an invitation to the state track meet and some pretty intense competition.

Whatever It Takes

The relay team {which she ran the first leg for) also qualified for state.

The level of competition 'got to her' and she didn't do as well as she had expected to at state. She was disappointed in herself until I reminded her that it was an honor and a privilege to get as far as she did as a freshman. I also explained to her that she now knew what to expect at this level of competition and that next year we would be back [at state] and she would "kick butt!". I was very proud of Tasha that day, and amid her tears, I shared my feelings of pride with her.

As a family, we were looking forward to summer.

Denny had just started a new job in county road maintainance and was able to spend alot more time at home. As a family project we added a deck to the back of our home and dug a pond [complete with a duck] to enhance our growing flower garden in the back yard. We attended the annual Butterfield Trail Ride the first weekend in June.

Cole and Denny were preparing for wheat harvest and to add a little more chaos, I was taking on the responsibility of managing the local restaurant beginning June 21. I had alot of preparation to do before opening day.

Dayna Gfeller-Mackley

Everything was falling into place perfectly. Even Tasha got a new summer job which she would start on June 21 too.

Saturday morning, June 19, 1999, we rose early. Denny went to the field to run the tractor and I headed to the restaurant to begin cleaning and painting. I hired a cleaning service to come in on Sunday morning to shampoo the carpet so I needed to have everything done by Saturday night. If everything went as planned I would be ready to open for business Monday at lunch time.

Tasha, Jenna and Tori arrived later in the morning to help clean and paint. Cole ran the loader, filling in holes in the parking lot with dirt. When he finished he headed south to spend the weekend with his girlfriend, Linsey and her family. We all worked very hard to accomplish what we had set out to do.

With the major part of the work complete, at 4 PM Tasha asked to go home and get ready to go out with her good friend Dallas. I continued working, hoping to finish around ten o' clock.

As I was finishing, Denny stopped in to see how everything was coming along. Tasha, Dallas and their friend, Cody arrived to check out the progress as well. It was hard to believe that everything was about ready for business.

Before she left around ten o' clock, I reminded Tasha to be home early-that I was exhausted and I didn't want to wait up too late for her to come home. We agreed on an 11:30 curfew. The three teenagers drove away and Denny and I headed home.

After showering, eating a late dinner and getting Jenna and Tori put to bed, I sat down to go over some paper work while I waited for Tasha to come home. I have never been able to sleep until all my children were home safely for the night. I knew Cole was spending the night at Linsey's, so Tasha was the only one keeping me from going to bed.

My dear, dear Tasha...she has always been my most challenging child. My most stubborn and strong willed, and always the one to "push the limits" of my patience. She continually broke curfew, coming home late {even if it was only a few minutes}. She knew she would pay the consequences the next weekend by staying home with mom and dad -"grounded". This had even become the joke amongst friends and family members. However, this was two weeks in a row out on the town! The previous weekend she went out with Cole and he made sure he kept her from any mischief.

Dayna Gfeller-Mackley

As 11:40 P.M. {ten minutes past curfew} approached, I was already mentally preparing my "you're grounded" lecture. I had made up my mind that at midnight I would pull on my jeans and go retrieve Tasha as I had before. At five till twelve, my sister in law was standing in my kitchen telling me of a car accident. She said "Dallas wrecked his car." Without hesitation, I responded, "Oh my God! Tasha was with him. Did you bring her home?". She replied, "No...she's gone." She had died instantly at the scene.

Forever, as long as I live, and probably long after, I will never forget that moment in time. I felt so many emotions. My first thought—- "Gone!?—-Impossible!"

Only two hours before, she was standing so near me (right next to me) that I could smell the scent of her freshly shampood hair. "Gone...How could she be gone?" She promised that she would be home at 11:30. She knew how tired I was. And besides that, I never got to tell her good-bye, to tell her one last time- just how much I love her, to tell her how fortunate I am to be the one chosen to be her mother. She couldn't be gone! Not yet! I am not finished being her mother! And we had made so many plans!

I went to the bedroom, woke Denny from a deep sleep and explained to him the horrible ordeal that seemed too bizarre to be even half way real.

Whatever It Takes

The next thing I did was call the one person I knew I could count on: Uncle David {my dad's younger brother}, the closest thing to a father I have ever known. Aunt Judy answered the phone. She thought someone was playing a sick, cruel joke until I convinced her it was me and *it* was true. They both came to our home immediately.

Next, I knew I had to call Cole. I had to tell him before someone else did. It was past midnight when Linsey's mother answered the phone. I explained what had happened. She said they'd wake Cole and drive him home. She also said she couldn't tell him Tasha had died. She told Cole that Tasha had been hurt in a bad accident and that he was needed at home.

He knew better. Thirty minutes later, when he arrived home, he came to me in my bedroom.

He told me,"I know she's dead."

When I asked how he knew, he replied…"Mother, I know you…If one of us are hurt, you aren't going to be shut up in your bedroom at home-you're going to be with us-where ever we are." He hugged me.

Cole also said it was apparent that she was dead when they turned the corner to our street and there were cars lining the street to our house. So many people had come to be with us.

At this point, I still hadn't cried. I was scared. I was numb. I felt sick to my stomach. I felt very alone, even though my house was full of people. How was I ever going to pull everyone through this one?

Our house, the yard, and the new deck were full of people who had arrived to offer comfort.

I closed the door to Jenna and Tori's room. They were sleeping. [After all it was 2:30 in the morning. Most ordinary and normal families should be sleeping. I was slowly beginning to realize...I wasn't in the classification of a"normal family".] The girls were asleep and I didn't want them to wake yet...Not until I knew how I was going to tell them that their big sister, Tasha, the one they idolized and looked up to, was dead..... forever.

Around 4 a.m. the last of our visitors finally left. Jenna and Tori, fortunately, were still sleeping. Cole and Linsey went to bed. Denny fell asleep right away. I was exhausted, but I couldn't sleep. Everytime that I shut my eyes I heard *things.* I heard tires squealing, metal crushing, glass shattering and kids screaming. I heard my daughter crying for help. Or I thought and imagined I heard my daughter

Whatever It Takes

crying for help. I couldn't establish what was 'real' and 'not real' anymore.

After nearly an hour of tossing and turning, I got up, straightened up the house and found myself in our pickup 'driving around' —-no where. Somewhere. Anywhere.

I found myself six miles north of town. At the curve. Where *it* happened. I began searching the area, thinking maybe there had been a mistake. Maybe Tasha wasn't dead. Maybe she was still there, waiting. ..waiting for me to come help her. After all, I am her mother and she thought I could fix anything!

It was extremely foggy and damp. With the aid of headlights, I could see tracks in the grassy ditch, probably where rescue workers and ambulances had entered and exited. I saw glass-lots of shattered glass. And I saw blood. Later, I would find out that it was Tasha's blood. It [the blood] would prove the exact location where the life drained from her body-*where she was when Jesus arrived to take her to heaven.*

Being there, all of a sudden something changed…I was scared-so scared and so very cold. I needed to go home. Home: where everything was safe and warm and protected. When I arrived home things were no different. It was still scary and cold, and ... Tasha's bed was still empty. I was lost! Even in my own home.

I made coffee and I showered. Jenna and Tori were waking. In the aftermath of everything that had happened during the night, I had totally forgotten that it was Father's Day-the day that our girls hold as high in reguards as Christmas. They were so excited! And with every reason...when they fell asleep hours earlier all was well. They assumed it still was.

Tasha, with the assistance of Jenna and Tori, had picked out "the perfect gift" for their daddy. They could hardly wait to present it to him.

Denny and I searched each others' eyes for a clue as to what to do next. We agreed...let them have their moment of happiness, giving daddy his gift-then we will share the news that will change their lives forever.

We told them of the accident and that Tasha was in heaven. They both cried. They asked questions, for which we had no answers. It was obvious: we had a long, long road ahead of us. It was then that the "control freak" in me decided, once again...I will do what ever it takes to get my family through this.

Whatever It Takes

Sunday morning. Eight hours after *the accident.* It started all over again. The people… everyone seemed to be flooding into our house. I know they mean well, they mean to help-but nothing can help. At one point I escaped into our garage and sat alone in my parked car just to get away from everyone. I pondered the thought of how I was going to spend a day [not a lifetime], just a day, without Tasha in it.

That sad Sunday passed. Monday morning arrived and with it, some emotions I was not expecting. I was sitting at the table eating a cinnamon roll someone had dropped off, waiting for Tasha to join me for breakfast like any other morning. Every other morning she would have teased me about the hair do that my pillow had created while I slept. But, not today. It was then that I cried for the first time. I was never going to see her smile or feel her touch again. Not since Friday afternoon, had I heard her say the words "I love you Mom". I would never hear it again. Not in this lifetime.

I cried while I ate. I cried while I cleared the dirty dishes. I cried in the shower and while getting dressed. I couldn't stop.

It was then that I felt the need to go to the funeral home. I needed to see her. I needed to make sure that they hadn't made a mistake. I needed to be sure it was her that was killed, even though I hoped that someone had made a mistake.

I told Denny I was going to town. He asked me "which town?" and "for what?". He knew where I was going and he knew why. He offered to drive me so I didn't have to go alone, but he said he didn't want to go in-he didn't want to see *it*.

Denny drove me to Oakley (23 miles) to the mortuary and waited in the car while I walked to the entrance and rang the bell. It took {what seemed like} forever for someone to come to the door. A lady appeared and I began to explain who I was when she interupted and said "I know who you are- go home and come back later. Tasha isn't ready yet."

I insisted and more or less told her that Tasha is my daughter and I wasn't going anywhere until I got to see her.

After much pleading, I was led to a dark room in the basement where a lifeless body lay on a table covered with a white sheet. I recall feeling sick, but yet, feeling 'out of my body'. The whole ordeal still seemed too bizarre to be real life.

The last thing I remember hearing was "Please remember, all the damage that you are about to see was done in three to five seconds." Then the funeral director

Whatever It Takes

pulled back the sheet and revealed my daughter. There had been no mistakes, it was Tasha... her teeth... her fingernails.

My first thought was "My God! How this had to have hurt!" I felt helpless and useless. As Tasha's mother, I wanted to fix everything and make her better. Every part of her was broken. Her beautiful face-destroyed. I bent to kiss her cheek only to make another part of her face fall away. I had never witnessed such destruction in all my thirty six years. I must had spent over an hour alone with her when the funeral director asked through the closed door if he could come in and talk to me.

We discussed some of the injuries and what could be done before the closed-casket service in three days. All I knew is that it was not acceptable [to me] to send my daughter to heaven looking like *this*, even if the bible does say that 'all things are new again in heaven'. (Revelation 21:5)

I spent the next two days at the mortuary. When the funeral director and I lifted Tasha's body into her casket, everything that could be fixed was fixed. I had even polished her fingernails and her toe nails with one of her favorite pastel colors. As I lowered myself to kiss her good bye one last time in that dark basement room, I felt an unearthly peace and in my own mind I imagined her saying "Thank you Mother, I know how difficult this was for you".

Many people frowned upon what I did and freely voiced their opinions. I heard what they said. Some said I was a morbid person for choosing to prepare my dead daughters' remains for burial. For those people, I feel sorry. And I wish that they would not judge me without walking a day in my shoes. If I had to do it all over, I would change nothing, as I know I did only what Tasha would have expected me to do. I did it for her. And I did it for me, as I knew there were going to be no more prom nights to help her get ready for. And I knew there would never be a wedding day that I would help her dress for. Not only that…I know that Tasha was no longer in her earthly body-she was watching me from above. I firmly believe that ones' soul and spirit leaves the body upon death. What is left behind is merely the package that we're wrapped in while on earth. *II Corinthians 5:8 When we are away from the body, we are at home with the Lord.*

After talking it over, Denny and I thought it was extremely important for Cole, Jenna and Tori to view Tasha's body. I was afraid that if we didn't allow them to see

Whatever It Takes

her one last time, they would always question whether or not it was Tasha's body beneath the lid of her casket.

The events of days between Saturday night and Thursday morning's funeral service are somewhat of a blur. Shock is a way of blocking out the intense pain and heartbreak that arrive with grief. It also blocks out everything else. I remember lots of people, lots of crying and lots of food. However, every minute spent at the funeral home and in the presence of Tasha's body is very clear and certain to me. I recall every thought and movement, each conversation between the funeral director and myself. Every detail. I even remember her smell. It is forever lodged somewhere in my memory.

There were a few incidences which occurrred in the days following Tasha's death which hurt Denny and I, Cole, Jenna and Tori tremedously. It' s almost funny...How at a time when you really need the love and support of the people closest to you, they are the one's who are sometimes [unknowingly] the most hurtful. I have forgiven these people for the hurt they caused, but I will not forget what they did. I figure their 'insensitivities' were based on stupidity and the shear lack of knowledge and understanding of what it feels like to lose a child. Many can try to imagine what it is like, but can never ever come close unless they experience the loss personally. It totally amazes me how kind, caring and compassionate some people can be and how insensitive and self-centered others can be in such a situation.

As her mother, I thought Tasha's funeral service was perfect...if it is possible for a funeral to be perfect. It was just as I had planned. It was a celebration of her life, not her death. It was a presentation of who she was-a teenager, not perfect by any means. A true committment to the person that God intended Tasha to be when He created her. An individual approached me after the service and told me he had never been to a more moving funeral service ever. He went on to say that when the service ended-he still wanted to hear more.

After the funeral and graveside service, I was finally ready to sleep. I felt mentally, emotionally, and physically exhausted, but sleep wouldn't come. There was plenty to do while I was awake, so I wrote thank you acknowledgements, sorted through the flowers and gifts that had accumalated in the house over the past several days, and there were many, many cards to still open and read. I also had a headstone to design and present to the company that would be engraving it. Within a week I had lost 20

Whatever It Takes

pounds and I couldn't afford to lose any more weight. You would think that with all the food carried into our house that I would put the pounds on, not shed them!

Denny came up with the idea that we all needed a vacation. Uncle David and Aunt Judy own a cabin in the mountains of New Mexico. In July Denny and I, Cole and Linsey, and Jenna and Tori joined them at the cabin for a peaceful vacation. It did everyone good to get away from everything at home for a while. However, for me, personally, being at the cabin only made losing Tasha more of a reality. For I knew how she enjoyed all the fun times she spent at the cabin as a young girl.

After almost a week, we returned home only to find that the hurt and pain of Tasha's death was still lurking in every aspect of our lives. All her things were still just as she had left them in our home. Her blue car was still parked in our driveway with all her little momentos still in it. Her jacket still hung on the coat rack at the back door. Even the blue sticky note she left hanging on the refrigerator door the night she died still claimed it's spot.

The note read:

Mom,

I'm with Dallas around town.

Talk to ya later.

Love Ya,

Tasha

Little reminders remain, like the last sour-dough pretzel that she had forbid anyone else to eat (because it was for her) was still wrapped in cellophane, resting on the freezer shelf. It still remains there, unwrapped, uneaten.

Life is supposed to go on. Looking around-everyone else's had. Mine hadn't.

Somedays it was even hard to breathe, not alone worry about taking care of a family and actually functioning. Many days I thought it would be easier to just stay in bed and pull the covers over my head.

I was also, slowly, finding out who my *real* friends were and weren't. The people that I had always thought were my friends said they couldn't understand me or couldn't 'deal ' with *it*. They said to give them a call when the old Dayna returned. I couldn't bear to tell them that the old Dayna died when Tasha died, as did all the hopes and dreams I had for her. There were going to be no more trackmeets, volleyball or basketball games, no more fun mother-daughter shopping trips and no more evening walks together. I also realized that there would be no graduation from high school or college. No wedding day, no son in

Whatever It Takes

law, no grandchild from Tasha to hold in my arms for the first time.

My real, true friends accepted me, as well as all the emotions and feelings that I carried with me. They were always available to listen, talk, hold my hand, or cry with me. I now realize what special friends I have been blessed with.

Come July, I had made up my mind to "suck it up" and get on with life, even if that meant smiling on the outside while I was crying on the inside. Jenna and Tori were having a difficult time too, especially if I let them get too tired. I kept them entertained with trips to the pool, lots of activities with their friends and frequent "girls' night out" in which we would go out to dinner and to a movie.

They would find comfort and smile when I would read to them from the bible about heaven. Slowly they were beginning to release some of the hurt, but always still talking of Tasha every day, remembering times together and sharing stories of their adventures with her.

On July 31, Cole and Linsey had been to Hays for the day. Linsey had a bridal shower to attend and Cole was going to use that time to buy her a birthday gift, her birthday being four days later. To my surprise, they came home sporting an engagement ring on Linsey's finger. They announced their wedding date: July 29, 2000.

I was so happy for them. Happy to see Cole healing and moving forward, I silently wished that it could only be that simple for me. I couldn't pick a more suitable wife for him myself. Linsey, as well as her family, had been by our side throughout the painful events of Tasha's passing. They had already become our family.

Before I knew it, the beginning of a new school year was approaching. I had no idea this would be so hard for me.

The first day of high school volleyball practice started and Tasha missed it! A week later, as the first day of school came and went I found myself getting angry and irritable. I wanted to shout "whoever has my daughter...would you please bring her home now?"

It hurt so badly to watch all her friends go to school, drag Mainstreet in their cars and, in general, live life without her. In my opinion, I thought they should cancel volleyball season because Tasha couldn't participate.

I did conjure up enough strength from somewhere to make an appearance at the teams' first volleyball match. It

Whatever It Takes

was very difficult. I fought back tears all evening. Later, a parent of one of the girls on the team expressed how important it was to the team that I was there. After that, I attended every game except two. I hated it but I guess I felt that I had something to prove to everyone (who thought that I couldn't do it).

During the final game of regional competition I had to get up and leave during the final match. It suddenly became very aware to me that the girls had a great chance of advancing to state and it hurt me to think that Tasha was missing her chance at it. I wanted *her* team to do well- but not just yet. It was too soon (for me). The team ended their season, losing during finals at substate.

The next milestone to approach: Tasha's 16 th birthday on October 4, 1999. It wasn't as sad as I let myself imagine that it would be. I took roses to her grave at the cemetery. It was apparent that many many friends had visited her grave that day in rememberance of her. That made me very happy to know that she wasn't forgotten.

My sister-in-law had bought a large poster of one of Tasha's favorite bible verses (Phillipians 4: 8&9)and had it laminated. She attached a permanent marker so everyone could sign it like a giant birthday card. At the end of the day it was covered with signatures and words of love for Tasha.

*When she was alive, every year on October 4, Tasha hosted a slumber party, inviting 8-10 friends. We would park the motor home in the driveway and they would have all the luxuries of home (except that parents, and boys, of course, were not allowed).

On this first birthday after Tasha's death, all the girls that had been (at one time or another) invited to one of Tasha's birthday/slumber parties, showed up at our house after school. Even a few that had never experienced one of those 'all-nighters' came. We ate homemade pizza and birthday cake just as we had done when Tasha was alive. We had a birthday party for Tasha and I know in my heart that she attended!

One Friday in December, I came home from work and changed into my "game sweatshirt" to go and support the girls basketball team like I always had before. A couple of hours later when Denny came home I was still dressed in my game shirt, depressed and crying. Figuring that I would go as I always did, he asked why I wasn't at the game. I remember giving him the most simple answer- "I don't have anybody to watch". Just because my daughter wasn't playing, I felt so out of place, like I didn't belong there. I didn't go to a game all season. I missed the excitement of attending the games, but I knew I couldn't bear to watch the girls play Tasha's favorite sport with her absent.

I was also noticing that instead of time healing my hurt- it was growing deeper and more painful with each day, for each day brought another scene of events without Tasha in it.

As the holidays approached, I could feel myself getting overly anxious, nervous and depressed. Denny's family decided to spend Christmas in Wichita at a hotel. I was so worried how Denny and our children would handle our first Christmas without Tasha. It would be our first Christmas without Tasha and our last Christmas with Cole living at home. Denny and I discussed it and we both felt we needed to keep everything as normal as possible. We would celebrate Christmas at home, alone with our children-not in Wichita.

Thank goodness for Uncle David and Aunt Judy, once again. They made sure we weren't alone for Christmas. And believe it or not, Christmas <u>was</u> almost normal! There were a few sad moments as everyone took the time to remember their favorite Christmas memories of Tasha. We enjoyed celebrating Christ's birthday, knowing thatTasha was spending her first Christmas with Him.

The new mellinium appeared without any major mishaps as many had feared. I, myself, was looking forward to a new century, thinking that it had to be better than the last one.

2000! Wow! I am quite sure that Tasha assumed she would be present for the turn of the century. I thought she would! It only proves that God's plans are not always what we would plan for ourselves.

With the new year-came a whole new mess of emotions. <u>Most</u> would assume that when a loved one dies the worst is over when the funeral ends. <u>Most</u> would be wrong.

Six months after Tasha's death would have to mark my lowest point. It was an awful experience. I felt like I was at the bottom of a deep dark hole and the harder I tried to climb out - the more I buried myself. I knew I was in trouble and I knew that I needed to get help. I admitted that I couldn't cry alone anymore. I thought that if I pretended that everything was OK-it would be OK. I would never let my emotions or feelings escape in the company of Denny or the children and expose them to anymore hurt or my pain.

Whatever It Takes

They all believed that if I was OK, then everything would be fine.

At this point I was experiencing horrible nightmares and severe depression. I was exhausted physically, mentally and emotionally. In this condition I was no good to my husband, my children or myself. And for the first time in my life, I really truly missed my mom and dad-which confused me even more. During a counselling session a doctor asked me "When else did you need your parents more?" He assured me that my feelings were normal. ....Normal...I can't remember the last time I felt normal.

With January 2000 being documented as my lowest point, I was gratefully looking forward to getting 'happier' again.

My doctor suggested a combination of "talk therapy" and prescribed medications to help me sleep at night and to regulate the chemical imbalance in my brain (my doctor explained this to be caused by years of suppressed emotional trauma and too much recent stress). I wasn't crazy after all!

It was always my belief that depression was a character flaw, something that you chose to be, not something that you have no control over. I saw it as a weakness. After being diagnosed with clinical depression, I learned that it is a real illness that can be treated. However, I wasn't ready to share with anyone that I was having difficulty coping with the life situation that I was living. At first I didn't even tell Denny or my children that I was seeking help or that I had been put on medication. As I mentioned, my family has learned to totally rely on the idea that "as long as mom is OK, we're all going to be fine". I couldn't let them down and take away their sense of security they find within me.

I had no where to go but up! I started counseling at this time and also changed churches and began attending Sunday services regularly.

With Cole and Linsey's wedding approaching in less that six months, there was alot of work to preoccupy my thoughts. Linsey was already an assett to our family. She made sure to include me in every decision regarding the wedding.

An especially fun day was the trip we took to Hays to try on wedding dresses. Linsey and her mother, sister and neice along with Jenna, Tori and myself spent the day trying on dresses and ordering accessories for the big day. It was a treat to watch Tori and Jenna trying on wedding veils right beside Linsey and laughing as they viewed their reflections in the mirror. For a few hours that afternoon their emotions seemed to disappear behind a wall of happiness. Jenna and Tori were finding a "sister" within Linsey and they were beginning to heal.

In many details of the wedding, Cole and Linsey were incorporating little inuendos reflecting memories of Tasha. Memories of Tasha were in the special selection of songs, the flower arrangements and even a special angel chosen to adorn the alter.

The week of the wedding arrived before I was ready. The night before rehearsal, Cole and I were in his room packing all of his belongings into boxes and suitcases for the move into his own home with his new life. I felt tears well up in my eyes as I began to experience some familiar emotions. Less than a year earlier, I was packing away some of Tasha's things after she had died. I was having those same feelings once again as I helped Cole pack. I asked him,"Cole aren't you sad that you are leaving home, leaving your life with your sisters and Dad and I behind?" He turned and looked at me with the biggest smile and a look of excitement in his eyes and he said "Mother, I'm not leaving you, and I'm not sad. I've never been happier. I am so excited to be moving out on my own and starting a whole new life with Linsey". I think it was at that exact moment when it became clear to me…I am certain that is what dying must be like. Imagine that the dying person is 'starting a whole new life'. What if the deceased is happy to move on to this new phase of life in eternity? Those who are left behind see it only as 'losing' them. We who are left behind are sad and grieving while those who have died may very well be moving on to a new, more exciting part of life, experiencing only happiness and pure joy.

This is probably one of the most enlightening conversations I had ever had with my son. I did know, however, that letting him go was going to be extremely hard. I don't think I could have made the adjustment had he married anyone but Linsey. I don't believe that I could have chosen a better daughter in law myself! She is not only my son's wife- she is one of my best friends.

The wedding was perfect, yet bittersweet. I couldn't help but wonder what it would have been like if our 'whole' family could have been present. When it came time for family pictures, I felt that someone was missing- I think I always will.

The next few weeks would bring another adjustment for our family. We all missed Cole's daily presence in our

Whatever It Takes

home. Jenna and Tori especially missed him. Overnight, Jenna became the oldest child in the family-always before she had been second to youngest. Tori finally got her own room, which at first disrupted her sleeping habits.

It was at this time that Denny and I shared a conversation that I am sure most parents never think about. We both admitted being very thankful that we had made the decision to 'have' Jenna and Tori. From the very beginnning of both pregnancies everyone else had done nothing except make negative comments and express discouraging thoughts at our announcement to expand our family. Only Denny and I could understand our need for a larger family. We feel that Jenna and Tori are God's most precious gift to us…to help us through the difficult trials that only He knew we would [one day] be going through. Had we not concieved Jenna and Tori, we would, in fact, be living with no children in our home at a very young (36 & 38) age [when we needed children most].

Most days, we are extremely happy that we went against everyone else's wishes and advice when they told us to "quit having children and setting yourself up for even more heartache".

To those people I say "HA! We knew what we were doing!"

God does indeed have plans for each of us! *Jeremiah 29:11——"For I know the plans I have for you" declares the Lord. "Plans to prosper you, not to harm you. Plans to give you hope and a future."*

I was becoming well aware of God's plan for me. Why else would God subject me to death so often if He didn't want me to learn from it and use it in some productive way. ** II Corinthians 1:3&4 —-God always gives us comfort when we are in trouble so we can share that comfort with others in trouble.*

I was developing strong urges to comfort other parents also coping with the loss of a child. I was also experiencing some unwanted spiritual feelings.

After Tasha's death there seemed to be an epidemic of fatal incidences in our area involving kids her age and younger. Everytime I would hear the tragic news of another death of someone's child I would have "sympathy pains". I would get the same sick feeling in the pit of my stomach and experience the same emotions-in a sense, returning to the night I learned of Tasha's death. I didn't even have to know the child or the parents and I still grieved for them.

One time for example: Seven months after Tasha's death, there was another accident in which a teenage girl

Whatever It Takes

had died in a car wreck. In my head I was consistently hearing a voice saying *"At least send this mother a sympathy card-no one knows better than you, what she is feeling at this time"*.

After weeks of ignoring 'the voice', I addressed an envelope and signed the card to send to this mother that I had never met before. What seemed like minutes later, I was proofreading a 3 page letter that I had written to her, sharing some of my experiences of heartache. I was somewhat amazed (and impressed) with this letter I had written. For in it were words and phrases that I would not normally utilize in daily conversation. I mailed the letter.

Later that day, a Christian friend phoned me to suggest that I write this mother a letter. I shared my feelings about the unfamiliar words I had written and sealed inside the card. She assured me that everything would be fine. She also assured me that those unfamiliar words were not mine. More likely than not, they were God's words. He was using me as a vessell to reach out to a grieving mother. I was becoming more comfortable with God's plans for me.

*Today, the grieving mother is a good friend of mine.

I never would have imagined aquiring such genuine friends through my daughter's death.

Unfortunately, the months to follow would bring many more opportunites for me to share my experiences with death.

So many accidents, so many deaths, so many young people. It is such a waste to see young, vibrant kids' lives haulted in only seconds because of poor judgement and unforseen, freak accidents. With each death I am reminded of how fragile life is and how short our time in this world actually is. With each death it is also very apparent that I am healing. As I spend time with a new grieving parent-I am amazed that I am no longer in that 'place' where he/she is. I am no longer 'fresh' in the grief and the deep, dark, painful emotional state that the shock of losing your child creates. I don't know when recovery happens. Healing *must* happen so gradually, an increment each day, that you aren't even aware that it is happening.

I still remember the evening that Dalton died like it was an hour ago. I hear every word exchanged in the ICU and recall every thought visible in the eyes of his attending physicians. I recall the stinging words informing me of Tasha's untimely death-the intense hurt in my heart and the sickening lump in the pit of my stomach. The difference between those two moments and today... I can move forward now. I know that it is in the past and it is something

Whatever It Takes

that I cannot change. It is something that I have left in God's hands, because I, myself, cannot carry those burdens any longer.

*I Peter 5:7 ——Cast all your cares upon Him, for He cares for you.

*Matthew 11:28 ——If you are tired from carrying heavy burdens, come to Me and I will give you rest.

I have learned to trust God, knowing that everything that occurs in my life is all part of His grand plan and that He doesn't intend to hurt us.

I have unknowingly started an informal support group in our area [for parents, such as myself], who are grieving the loss of a child. When I learn of the death of a child-I send a card along with a letter of support and offer any help I can give. I later follow up with a visit to their home or invite the parents to our home for dinner. I turn strangers into friends. I know that Tasha would be pleased-knowing that my commitment to her life didn't end when she died. Helping someone else to move forward in their life after such a traumatic event also helps me. For, as I try to help mend someone else's shattered heart, I tend to dwell less on my own.

Dayna Gfeller-Mackley

When Tasha died, many people spoke the usual words meant to bring comfort. One phrase in particular, meant to bring comfort, really offended me: "Something good will come of this, you'll see."

How dare someone say that to me? How could anything good come from my daughter's death, when she had so much yet to give? I would never trade her life [or anyone else's, for that matter] to see something good arise from the tragedy.

But...it is true...eventually, whether I like it or not, good things do come. I see little things everday.

For instance, in my three surviving children, I see how different they look at life-knowing that tomorrow is never certain. They value family so much more now than before *that day*. Each of us try to treat one another like it may be the last time to see them. Don't get me wrong-we still have our little disagreements and occassionally argue- but we never walk away leaving the situation unfinished.

Another positive aspect Tasha's death created was our family relationship with Christ. In searching for a way to cope with her death, we found a church, with a very gifted, down-to-earth pastor, that provides us with the understanding in what Jesus actually did when He suffered and died on the cross. We know that the only way to be reunited with loved one's that have passed before us, is to believe in God, Jesus, and salvation; and to live the way that God intended us to live. Our committment to our faith has been an enriching journey in our quest for healing. Tasha is responsible for that.

Also because of Tasha's death, I have met some really wonderful people. These new friends and myself have a common bond: each of us, through death, has unwillingly given up at least one child. We can comfort each other without ever speaking a word. There are times when holding someone's hand and crying with them says "I care" more than the most eloquent speech. I can gaze into the eyes of a grieving mother and know what her heart feels. We can finish each other's sentences because we know what it is like to have your child, an extension of you, gone forever.

I Timothy 1: 12: I thank Christ our Lord. He has given me the strength for my work because He knew that He could trust me.

Tasha's death has also made me a more compassionate person. I can no longer attend a funeral without thinking: "This is someones' child". It doesn't matter how old a person is…whether he/she is 2, 22, 52, or 72….if the parent survives, acknowledge that that parent is deeply scarred because of this child's death.

Many times I have looked on and been witness to a parent either emotionally or verbally picking their child apart. I want to tell them: "You know what-if I only had my daughter back, I would never say "I wish you would...." or "Why don't you ever...". If given one more chance, I would only cherish every moment I had left with her and love her for who she is. I would hug her one last time and tell her how much I love her and how privileged I feel to be chosen to be her mother.

I would suggest to every parent and child who don't get along or don't even speak to each other-"Don't wait until one of you die to start a relationship". I am so thankful for the relationship I had with Tasha and will always treasure the fun times and even the not-so-fun times that we were allowed to share.

Through good times and bad, it is quite apparent that life, without our approval, continues to go on. Denny and I recently became grandparents for the first time. Our grandson, Jace Colten Mackley, was born on April 9, 2002. His birth is a continual blessing to our family. This one small child is a gift from God that reminds us that life *does* go on.

Whatever It Takes

I was there when Jace was born. As I heard his strong cries I didn't know whether to laugh or to cry. A new life brings with it new hope, as well as new love. Despite what others may think, I know that nothing or no one could ever replace my children that have died, but when I first held little Jace in my arms, I knew that I had just been given "a little something" back. And until I held this child in my arms, I didn't know it was possible to love someone else's child as much as I love my own.

When Cole and Linsey first announced that they were expecting a baby, they told us that if it was a girl they would like to name her Tasha. In December, a sonogram revealed that the baby was a boy. I'll have to admit that I was a bit relieved. I would have cherished a grand-daughter, however, I personally thought that it was a bit to soon [for me anyways] for another Tasha!

When Cole first confided in me that they were ready to start their family, I was so happy for him, but at the same time I wanted to warn him. I wanted to say "Please don't do it…don't set yourself up for all the pain and heartbreak that loving a child can bring into your life". Then I reminded myself: *each* of my children have enriched my life with much more happiness, pleasant memories and personal fulfillment than anything, even their death, could ever diminish. I am very, very proud of each of my children.

I suppose if I had to sum up my entire life in just a couple of chapters, I would first have to say, most importantly, listen to God- He is always talking to you, waiting for you to listen. Personally, I think that if you don't listen when He speaks, He will allow drastic measures to occur in your life until, finally, He gets your attention and you are willing to listen to Him. In my case, I believe God has always had the same plan for me and my life, but I was always too busy living my life my way, too busy to listen for His instruction. He eagerly tried to get my attention several times, first when the twins were born. I should have been drawn to God then. Again, when He allowed Dalton's illness to progress. And yet again when Jesse was born premature. Even when Tori's life hung in the balance as a newborn, I questioned God's motives, but I never listened for his answer or advice. I never listened for His answer, or perhaps my heart was not *right* with God to perceive His answer. Who knows?......But when He allowed my Tasha to die, He got my attention. I had questions! And I demanded answers! I am learning to be patient and wait for

Whatever It Takes

answers. I am learning to recognize God's voice and to obey.

I hear him always when someones child dies. He says "Go to them, I have prepared you for this."

God doesn't give me answers as I ask for them. I think He tells me <u>what</u> I need to hear <u>when</u> I need to hear it.

One evening in particular, I was at home, alone in my bedroom. I was really tired and depressed (and I'll admit) feeling sorry for myself. I prayed. I asked God: "Why did my parents die? Why my three little boys? And why Tasha of all people, WHY?"

God immediately answered part of my question. He said "I didn't cause your parents to die. I allowed it to happen to make you a stronger person, enabling you to endure everything that would later burden you, to make you rely solely on Me and trust solely in Me."

God also asked me to do something else. He spoke of all the children who are estranged from their parents. He asked me to reach the kids who have good, honest, loving parents and to tell them not to wait until it is too late to try to have a relationship with them. He wants them to love, respect, and honor their parents as the bible says to do {Proverbs 6:20-22}. He told me that because I know what it is like to go through life 'longing' for my parents, I could do this.

I believe that God arranges everything in your life and places certain people in your life at just the right time. Looking back I can recall several times that I have crossed paths with strangers, and (today) the situations seem to be merely more that coincidences.

One particular time was in 1995 when Denny and I took a cruise to the Bahamas. On the second day on board the ship, I did as many of the passengers did-I got very seasick! I was laying down in the lower deck of the ship with all the other sick passengers. To pass time, an older gentleman (a retired doctor, who seemed to have taken a personal interest in my well-being) struck up a conversation with me. He brought me crackers and 7-UP and we talked. Throughout our four-hour conversation he asked me how many children we had, were we lived and other casual questions. Thinking I had all kinds of time to kill I thought "What the heck..." and I told him of Cole, Tasha, Jenna and Tori....and I told him about our three little boys who had died almost 10 years earlier. He, in turn, asked me many questions, one of them being "How do you ever get through the death of a child?".

Whatever It Takes

Voluntarily, I told him of some of the 'ups and downs' of my coping experiences. I also shared that one of the most comforting things I had discovered was reading books on death, the dying process, and hopes of eternity.

*Incidentally, on the way to the airport to embark on our vacation, I had just finished reading an excellent book on actual studies of near-death-experiences and life after life on earth. I explained the book to him in detail, shared my opinions about it, and went so far as to suggest that he read it someday. We shared some interesting views on the subject of death.

As the ship neared the coastline, my new friend and I closed our conversation and stood to our feet to go our separate ways. He extended his hand in an effort to shake my hand and he introduced himself by name…..He was the author of the book I had just explained to him and suggested that he read!!!! Merely a coincidence….I don't think so!

****

Life is all about living generously and creating something from what is handed to you. I have been so blessed! I've had a wonderful, wonderful life so far…a few rough times, but even those diffucult times have been a learning experience that has enriched my life in some meaningful way or another.

After my parents' death in 1965, the rest of my family made me, as a child, feel so loved and wanted that I never really missed having parents until I was well into my adult years, especially when Tasha died. Even at that time, my faithful family came to my rescue. They are such a blessing.

I made some wise choices too. I chose a terrific husband. He lets <u>me</u> be <u>me</u> and he tries so hard to understand what I'm going through, when I, sometimes, don't even understand myself.

I also *chose* to be a full-time stay-at-home mother. No college education, no fancy career or job title, just a mom. And I am so very thankful for my children. They *are* my life. They are good kids, with so much love and respect. They are the best thing I have ever done! I think my parents would be very proud of them.

And last, but not least, one of my smartest choices…I finally chose to listen to God when He speaks. The hurdles placed in my race of life have, most definitely, made me a stronger, wiser person and did draw me closer to the Lord.

He does have a plan for me. And I know that with Him I can do…

.... WHATEVER IT TAKES!

*Phillipians 4:13 —-With Christ all things are possible.

****

Can hardship and trials in your life actually be a blessing? I once read that fiery trials may be painful, but if by God's grace we endure them, our faith can emerge from the blazing furnace purer and stronger than it was before.

* I Peter 1: 6-7 ——-Have faith in God, whose power will protect you until the last day. On that day you will be glad, even if you had to go through many hard trials for a while. Your faith will be like gold that has been tested in a fire. These trials will prove that your faith is worth much more than gold which can be destroyed.

* Job 23:10 ——-When He has tested me, I shall come forth as gold.

The difficulties in our life provide the opportunity to show God's power and grace.

In coping with the death of my children, I especially found comfort in the words of truth that God speaks in the bible, describing heaven:

*Revelation 21: 4 & 5 ——I will wipe away all tears from their eyes, and there will be no more death, suffering, crying or pain. These things of the past are gone forever.

I make everything new again. My words are true and trusted.

About the Author

Dayna Gfeller-Mackley was born and raised in a quiet, small, rural community (population 200) in northwest Kansas. She was brought up and nurtured by loving family members after being orphaned at age two.

Dayna was a third-generation graduate from the local school system and married her high school sweetheart. Mrs. Mackley and her husband of twenty-two years are the proud parents of seven children and at the present time, have one grandson. As a first-time author, Dayna shares her joys in life, as well as the heartbreaking losses which have molded her into the woman she is today.

Printed in the United States
1052700001B/265-396